Life of Pi

Yann Martel

TEACHER GUIDE

NOTE:

The trade book edition of the novel used to prepare this guide is found in the Novel Units catalog and on the Novel Units website. Using other editions may have varied page references.

Please note: We have assigned Interest Levels based on our knowledge of the themes and ideas of the books included in the Novel Units sets, however, please assess the appropriateness of this novel or trade book for the age level and maturity of your students prior to reading with them. You know your students best!

ISBN 978-1-60878-110-2

To order, contact your local school supply store, or:

Toll-Free Fax: 877.716.7272
Phone: 888.650.4224
3901 Union Blvd., Suite 155
St. Louis, MO 63115

sales@novelunits.com

novelunits.com

Table of Contents

Skills and Strategies

Critical Thinking
Analysis, inferences, research,
opinions, predictions

Comprehension
Plot development, compare/
contrast, pros/cons

Literary Elements
Unreliable narrator, theme,
irony, humor, symbolism,
conflict, anthropomorphism

Vocabulary
Definitions, application

Listening/Speaking
Presentation, play, discussion

Writing
Essay, poetry, research paper,
letter, journal, synopsis

Across the Curriculum
Literature—*Robinson Crusoe,
The Old Man and the Sea,*
Aesop's Fables, book review,
author interview; Biology—
animal habitat needs,
carnivorous plants; Psychology—
defense mechanisms, fantasy vs.
reality, animal psychology; Art—
poster, photography, painting,
collage, comic

Genre: survival fiction

Setting: Pondicherry, India; Toronto, Canada; lifeboat in the Pacific Ocean; Tomatlán, Mexico

Point of View: multiple first person

Themes: death, self-preservation, loss, faith, love, truth, animal codependence and coexistence, survival skills, the value of storytelling

Conflict: person vs. society, person vs. self, person vs. person, person vs. nature

Style: detailed retrospective of survival, interspersed with journalistic commentary by the narrator (who is interviewing Pi Patel)

Tone: alternatively bleak and hopeful

Date of First Publication: 2001

Summary

Pi and Ravi Patel are the sons of a zookeeper in Pondicherry, India. Pi grows up learning the intricate details of animal behavior, behavior modification, and animal upkeep. Pi also finds great solace in his Hindu faith, though he eventually incorporates Christian and Islamic ideals. Political insecurities force Pi's father to sell the zoo and move his family to Canada. The Japanese ship they take from India, which also carries many of the zoo's animals, sinks in the Pacific Ocean. Pi is the sole human survivor, escaping in a lifeboat with an injured zebra, a hyena, an orang-utan, and a 450-pound Bengal tiger named Richard Parker. During the first few days, the animal population on the lifeboat is reduced to Richard Parker. Pi builds a raft out of oars and lifejackets, which he secures to the lifeboat so he can keep a safe distance from Richard Parker. Pi decides to keep the tiger alive due to the promise of companionship and Pi's peaceful, nonviolent nature. Eventually, Pi understands that the only way to survive is to train Richard Parker to be submissive. Using his vast knowledge of animals, Pi succeeds. By using the tools and supplies he finds aboard the lifeboat, Pi feeds himself and catches food for Richard Parker, surviving for months on meager rations, few tools, a strong determination to live, and prayer. As water and food become scarce, Pi loses his vision. Soon he hears a voice. At first, Pi thinks he has lost his mind, but then he realizes he has met another castaway, a blind Frenchman. Pi is overjoyed, but the French cook tries to kill Pi. Richard Parker intervenes and kills the Frenchman. Utilizing the paltry supplies on the Frenchman's boat, Pi regains his vision and drifts to a strange island composed entirely of vegetation and algae. The algae are edible and sweet, and they create large pools of fresh water inland. The island is also full of meerkats, supplying Richard Parker with food. Both castaways regain their strength, but Pi soon discovers that the island itself is carnivorous and that the algae become toxic to the touch at night. Realizing they cannot live on the dangerous island, Pi and Richard Parker return to the lifeboat and the Pacific Ocean. After another long bout of starvation, they arrive in Mexico. Richard Parker flees into the jungle without bidding Pi goodbye. Pi recovers at a hospital and tells his story to two disbelieving Japanese government agents. Pi then tells them another version of his story in which Pi survives with his mother, an injured Chinese sailor, and a French cook. The second story is much more brutal, and the two agents decide they prefer the first. Both versions of the tale are possible, leaving the reader to wonder which is true and whether the *manner* in which the truth is conveyed really matters at all.

About the Author

Yann Martel was born in Salamanca, Spain in 1963 to Canadian parents. As a child and as an adult, Martel traveled the world, visiting countries such as Iran, India, France, Mexico, Costa Rica, and Turkey. Before writing *Life of Pi,* Martel studied religious texts for two years and visited many temples and zoos in India. After working odd jobs and traveling, Martel began to write full time at age 27. His published works include *The Facts Behind the Helsinki Roccamatios* (1993), *Self* (1996), and *Life of Pi* (2001), which won the Man Booker Prize For Fiction in 2002. Since then he has published other short stories and *Beatrice and Virgil: A Novel* (2010). While Brazilian author Moacyr Scliar accused Martel of plagiarism, saying Martel copied his 1981 novel about a castaway in a boat with a jaguar, the two have reconciled, and Martel even thanks Scliar in the Author's Note in newer editions of *Life of Pi.*

Characters

(**Note to the Teacher:** Please be aware that there are two characters named Mr. Satish Kumar. It may be helpful to clarify this point to your class prior to novel discussion.)

Narrator: generally assumed to be a fictitious version of Yann Martel due to the various parallels with his life; makes numerous comments about the older Pi telling the story; This fictitious narrator, as well as the "Author's Note" on pages *v–xi* of the novel, is a plot device used to make the reader think this story is real.

Piscine "Pi" Molitor Patel: protagonist; 16-year-old son of a zookeeper; survives a sinking ship and spends eight months afloat in the Pacific Ocean, using his faith in God, his knowledge of animals, and the tools aboard his lifeboat; grows up to study religion and zoology in college; eventually finds a peaceful, happy life in Toronto, Canada

Richard Parker: a 450-pound Bengal tiger who accompanies Pi on his journey across the Pacific; learns to submit to Pi's commands after much training; escapes into a Mexican jungle; In Pi's alternate version of the journey, Richard Parker represents Pi's animal instincts and tenacious will to survive.

Santosh Patel: Pi's father; owns the Pondicherry Zoo; decides to sell the zoo and move his family to Canada after political unrest makes life in India unsatisfactory; dies when the ship sinks

Gita Patel: Pi's mother; dies when the ship sinks; In Pi's alternate tale, she survives with Pi but the French cook murders her.

Ravi Patel: Pi's older brother; loves to play cricket; dies when the ship sinks

Francis "Mamaji" Adirubasamy: a champion swimmer who teaches Pi to swim; His tales about pools and swimming in France inspire Pi's father to name Pi after a pool in France; meets the narrator in India and is the first to tell him about Pi's story

Mr. Satish Kumar: Pi's biology teacher, mentor, and friend; an avowed atheist and Communist

Mr. Satish Kumar: a Sufi; a Muslim mystic; teaches Pi about Islam

Father Martin: teaches Pi about Jesus and Christianity

French cook: another castaway adrift in the Pacific; tells Pi he is also blind, and after a long conversation, attempts to kill Pi but is eaten by Richard Parker; In Pi's alternate tale, the cook joined Pi, a Chinese sailor, and Pi's mother right when the ship sinks, and in this version, Pi kills the cook after the cook murders the sailor and Pi's mother.

Mr. Okamoto and Mr. Chiba: two agents of the Maritime Department in the Japanese Ministry of Transport who interview Pi about the sinking of the *Tsimtsum*; They do not believe his initial tale about surviving with a tiger for eight months, but when he tells them the alternate story without the tiger, they prefer to believe the first.

Background Information

The following information will enhance students' understanding of the novel.

The Castaway in Literature

A castaway is a surviving victim of a shipwreck or plane crash who lives by treading the ocean, drifting in a lifeboat, or living on a deserted island. Someone who is "marooned" is left behind on purpose, usually for punishment. Some famous castaways include Alexander Selkirk (whose story became the inspiration for *Robinson Crusoe*), Chunosuke Matsuyama (whose "messages in bottles" were found long after he died on a deserted island), Otokichi (a young Japanese boy who spent 14 months at sea), and Dougal Robertson (who survived for 38 days at sea after killer whales destroyed his ship). The story of the castaway is a popular tale in both literature and film.

The Emergency and Indira Ghandi

Pi's family leaves India during India's political struggles of the mid-1970s. "The Emergency" was a 21-month-long political struggle in India between 1975 and 1977. It involved President Ahmed and Prime Minister Indira Gandhi, who took over control of the Indian government and suspended all new elections. During this time, Indira Gandhi suspended many civil liberties, rewrote many laws to give her more power, and rooted out political opposition. She did so to control a nation in turmoil over security threats from Pakistan. The police arrested many protestors and political leaders. Indira Gandhi eventually allowed elections to take place in 1977, thus ending the "emergency." To this day, many debate the pros and cons of Indira Gandhi's choices to "improve" the nation. Some say she eliminated riots and gangs that harassed India through previous decades and that she drastically improved the nation's economy. Others say the government blatantly abused its powers in direct opposition to democratic values. Detainees were abused and tortured, thousands were arrested without trials or evidence, and the government forced surgeries upon men to prevent them from having children and to slow the population surge.

Bengal Tigers

Bengal tigers are native to India and parts of Southeast Asia. Many zoologists consider the Bengal tiger to be one of the largest tigers, and one of the largest "big cats," in the world, with most adults weighing in around or over 400 pounds. In some rare cases, they weigh over 600 pounds, and the record is currently 857 pounds. Tigers are solitary creatures that prowl and protect their territory. Females are less territorial but will fight fiercely if their territory is threatened. Bengal tigers eat only meat and hunt almost any animal in their territory, focusing their efforts on lone animals or those straying from a herd. Tigers will only hunt humans when humans disturb their hunting, wander into their territory, separate a mother from her cubs, or if they cannot find any other prey to hunt in their territory.

Initiating Activities

Use one or more of the following to introduce the novel.

1. On the page of the novel titled *"Praise for* LIFE OF PI," reviewers mention four other pieces of fiction: *Robinson Crusoe, The Old Man and the Sea,* Aesop's Fables, and the Calvin and Hobbes comic strip. Have students select one, research their selection, and write an essay discussing at least two major themes from their selected work that they think will also appear in *Life of Pi.* Students must explain why they believe these themes are important in their selected work and why they will be important in *Life of Pi.* After finishing the novel, students should also write a response to their own essay in which they revisit their initial predictions.

2. Instruct students to research other famous castaways and shipwreck survivors. Students may write an essay, create an oral presentation with visual aids, or utilize another creative media to address the following: how each survivor became a castaway, the duration and location of the castaway's survival, tools used or created, provisions s/he started with and/or acquired, how s/he was rescued, and (if possible) how his or her life changed because of the experience.

3. In the novel, Pi Patel states that it is easy to anthropomorphize animals, thus underestimating the dangers these animals may present to humans. Have students a) research anthropomorphism and explain what it means in their own words, b) select five random animals, explaining two ways in which our modern society has anthropomorphized them, and c) explain whether or not they consider Pi's warning valid.

4. Ask students to write an opinion essay responding to one of the following statements: a) A story does not need physical proof to verify its truth; b) People will believe what they want to hear and disbelieve what displeases them; c) A person can practice more than one religion at a time because, as Pi relates, "All religions are true" (p. 87); d) Animals prefer comfortable confinement to freedom to wander in unknown wilderness. Students must explain their opinions and support their opinions with examples.

5. Instruct students to research Hinduism, Christianity, and Islam and answer the following questions for each.

   a) How and with whom did this religion originate?

   b) What are this religion's core beliefs?

   c) Does this religion have any special practices or rituals? Describe three religious practices.

   After they have conducted their research, students should predict how religion will be important to the plot of *Life of Pi.*

Author's Note–Chapter 14

The novel opens with an "Author's Note," likely from the point of view of a fictional version of Yann Martel. Like Martel, the narrator visits India to write a novel but meets a man who tells him about Pi's story. The narrator travels back to Canada, finds Pi, and records the story, adding his own commentary throughout. Pi initially discusses his life in Canada and his successful academic career in religion and zoology. He also relates his childhood experience in India. He learns to swim at an early age, and explains how his father named him after a pool in France (a detail Pi's father gleans from Mr. Adirubasamy's stories about swimming in France). Children mock the name Piscine Molitor Patel, and when Pi moves to a new school, he takes the opportunity to give himself the nickname Pi (like the mathematic symbol). Pi gives a detailed account of growing up in a zoo, explaining animal psychology and the misconceptions people have about captive animals. His father teaches him to fear and respect all animals. Pi also learns how to gain an animal's respect through training and diligence, a skill that Pi will find vital later in the novel.

Vocabulary
anecdotes
exemplary
indolence
yogis
anemic
incessant
raiments
proffered
tremulous
intuitive
disrepute
strenuous

Discussion Questions

1. For what did the narrator initially go to India, and what did he find there? (*While having trouble finding the inspiration to finish his third novel, the narrator flies to India because "a stint in India will beat the restlessness out of any living creature; that a little money can go a long way there; and that a novel set in Portugal in 1939 may have very little to do with Portugal in 1939" [p. v]. He has beautiful visions of sitting upon a hill at a large table drinking tea in front of his notes. Unfortunately, his situation is not all that he envisioned, and his "novel sputtered, coughed and died" [p. vi]. He realized his story was "emotionally dead," and it left him with "an aching hunger" [p. vii]; The narrator meets Francis Adirubasamy, who tells him that he knows "a story that will make [him] believe in God" [p. ix]. The narrator is incredulous of this claim, but once he hears the details, he returns to Canada to find Pi Patel. While he went to India to find the inspiration to finish his novel, the narrator actually discovers a new story to write.*)

2. Discuss Pi's life in Canada. Did he initially adjust well to his new home? (*Pi loves Canada. Even though he misses many things about India, such as the heat, the food, the musicals, and the talk of cricket games, and even though Canada is "much too cold for good sense," it is "inhabited by compassionate, intelligent people" [p. 7] and he has found much success there. He enjoyed his academic career studying religion and zoology at the University of Toronto, narrowly missing some major awards for his work there, though he was a top student at St. Michael's College. He is married with a child, appears to be comfortably settled, and has a peaceful, compassionate attitude toward life. Pi's initial adjustment was difficult, as symbolized by an incident at the first Indian restaurant he visited in Canada. He dove into his food with his fingers and then was embarrassed as an amused waiter asked, "Fresh off the boat, are you" [p. 8]? Pi realized then that his adjustment was not going to be easy and that he had many un-westernized habits from his youth and lingering effects from his journey across the Pacific.*)

3. Pi's father ran a hotel before he ran a zoo. In what ways is running a zoo a hotelkeeper's worst nightmare? How did Pi feel about the zoo? (*Running a zoo is a hotelkeeper's worst nightmare because the "guests" are always in their rooms, expect full board, constantly have noisy and unruly visitors, are unsanitary, complain about the food and slow service, and are sexually depraved. Pi remembers the zoo fondly. Every day he saw things that were "both ordinary and unforgettable," [p. 18] and he felt rich because of these wonderful experiences.*)

4. What does Pi mean when he says, "Animals in the wild are, in practice, free neither in space nor in time, nor in their personal relations" (p. 20)? Do you agree with this statement? Why or why not? *(Pi is trying to explain his belief that animals are not free, even in the wild, and he thinks it is a fallacy that animals in captivity crave freedom and would be much happier in the wild. He believes that animals are content in captivity so long as all of their needs are met. Animals are "territorial" beings and crave the familiar, a place where they can fulfill their two greatest desires, to avoid enemies and find food and water, both of which they can achieve in a zoo. Animals will not wander simply out of curiosity because they fear the unknown. Pi states, "If a man, boldest and most intelligent of creatures, won't wander from place to place…why would an animal, which is by temperament far more conservative" [p. 20]? Pi gives many examples and explanations of this idea, even some that show how unwilling animals are to escape zoos, and though he does admit that bad zoos are unhealthy for animals, he feels zoos with proper caretakers, privacy, and space are very good places for animals to live their lives. Answers will vary.)*

5. How does Pi receive his name, and how does he change people's attitude about his peculiar name? *(Pi's father names him Piscine Molitor Patel after a swimming pool in France, a name he learns from Francis Adirubasamy, who was a champion swimmer. Francis tells Pi's father many tales from his days in Europe and eventually teaches Pi how to swim. Pi doesn't mind his name until boys at school begin to mock him. When Pi moves to a new school, he forms a plan to prevent teasing about his name. When it is his turn to introduce himself, he runs to the front of the room and writes on the blackboard "My name is Piscine Molitor Patel, known to all as Pi Patel" and adds "π = 3.14" for good measure. The new nickname quickly catches on.)*

6. In what ways does Pi describe "Man" as the most dangerous animals in the zoo? *(Pi explains that humans pose a threat to all other animals. He says there are always humans who will "feed fishhooks to the otters, razors to the bears, [and] apples with small nails in them to the elephants" [p. 36]. Pi goes on to list even more examples of animal cruelty, each one more bizarre and gruesome than the last. To make this point known to zoo visitors, Pi's father installed a sign in their zoo that read "DO YOU KNOW WHICH IS THE MOST DANGEROUS ANIMAL IN THE ZOO?" [pp. 38–39] beside a curtain, and behind the curtain was a mirror.)*

7. What is even more dangerous in a zoo than "Man," and how does Pi's father teach this to him? *(The most dangerous animal is "Animalus anthropomorphicus, the animal as seen through human eyes" [p. 39]. Humans see some animals as "cute" and "friendly" and others as "vicious" and "bloodthirsty," when really the animals can differ greatly from these widespread stereotypes. When humans do not understand an animal, they misjudge behaviors and misinterpret intentions, which can lead to dangerous situations. Pi's father tries to make his sons understand that all animals can be dangerous, so he feeds a goat to their Bengal tiger in front of them, which is a horrific display of power and carnage that the boys will never forget. Then he takes them through the zoo and explains how even the most ordinary animals can be pressed into defending their territory or fighting for dominance or food. Pi's father explains to his sons that they must view all animals cautiously with realistic eyes because "every animal is ferocious and dangerous" [p. 47].)*

8. Even though Pi states that most animals are not apt to escape, there are always situations that will drive an animal to extremes. According to Pi, what things might drive some animals to seek new habitats outside of their enclosures? *(Pi says, "Every animal has particular habitat needs that must be met" [p. 50] if they are to remain happy. The slightest change can upset animals and send them into a panic. This can happen if conditions in an enclosure are not just right or if any other variable is off. If any particular change occurs, an animal may attempt to escape to find a place with the right balance, though that place is not always in the wild. Many animals escape to populated areas where they do not belong, and they may hide for long periods of time before anyone*

finds them. A black leopard once escaped the Zurich Zoo and remained on the loose for over two months until it was found under a barn. The animal had nowhere to go and only attempted escape because of physical quarrels with other leopards. Pi states that "animals don't escape to somewhere but from something. Something within their territory has frightened them…and set off a flight reaction" [p. 51].)

9. According to Pi, what is the best way to train a "mighty predator" like a lion? *(Pi states that "a circus trainer must always enter the lion ring first" [p. 54] for two reasons—so the trainer is not invading the lions' territory and to claim the territory for himself first. The trainer reinforces his dominance through his actions. The lions realize they are in the presence of an alpha-male and stay to the edges of the ring. They understand that this alpha-male keeps them busy and feeds them regularly, so they do as he says. The trainer must never slip up or lose his rank because social rank determines everything about a lion's life. Training a lion is "a question of brain over brawn" [p. 55], and the trainer must retain his authority at all times.)*

10. **Prediction:** In what ways will Pi's experience living at the zoo help him later in the novel?

Supplementary Activities

1. Select an animal, and research the type of habitat it would require to live in a zoo. Create a list of specific needs, and design a living space for the animal. You may use maps, pictures, and designs from other famous zoos to help create your own habitat, but be sure to explain what makes your habitat unique.

2. Use the Word Map on page 31 of this guide to find information about six vocabulary words from this section.

3. Use the Pros and Cons chart on page 32 of this guide to list the positive and negative aspects of having an unusual name.

Chapters 15–36

Pi is born and raised as a Hindu, but his religious curiosity compels him to investigate Christianity and Islam. He practices all three, firmly believing that "religion is more than rite and ritual" (p. 60) and that all three are connected by shared philosophies and core desires for peace, love, and devotion to something greater than the individual. Pi's devotion to all three faiths leads to trouble, and people begin to ask questions. Church officials from all three groups come to speak to Pi at the zoo, and all are shocked to hear of Pi's devotion to the other's faith. Pi tries to explain that each faith brings him joy and that there is nothing wrong with being a member of each. His parents, though perplexed, support his decision. Pi asks each of his parents if he can be baptized and have an Islamic prayer rug, and he receives both. After political unrest in India frustrates Pi's father, he decides to sell the zoo and move to Canada.

Vocabulary
sanctified
intolerable
avatar
petulant
exaltation
askance
apoplectic
esplanade
depravity
precarious
memorabilia
incredulous

Discussion Questions

1. Describe Pi's apartment in Canada. What do you think this says about his religious and philosophical beliefs? *(As the narrator says, Pi's home "is a temple" [p. 56]. Artifacts, symbols, and books from almost every major religion fill his walls and shelves, including pictures of Ganesha and the Virgin Mary and a photo of the "black-robed Kaaba, holiest sanctum of Islam" [p. 57]. Pi also has pictures of Krishna, a stone Shiva yoni linga, a small conch shell, and "a wooden Christ on the Cross" [p. 58], among other items. Answers will vary, but some may see this type of religious diversity as a sign that Pi is deeply spiritual but is not bound by any particular dogma. He is the type of person who finds inspiration from a range of beliefs and finds solace in their shared core values.)*

2. What belief system does Pi follow first, and why is it so important to him? *(Pi is born into the Hindu faith. He is taught the religion by his parents, who are Hindus that are not particularly devout. Pi says he feels that things make sense to him through the lens of Hinduism. He says he owes "to Hinduism the original landscape of [his] religious imagination" [p. 63].)*

3. How does Pi discover Christianity, and what initially confuses him about the faith? *(When Pi is 14 years old, he visits Munnar. On the three hills around Munnar there are a Christian church, a Hindu temple, and an Islamic mosque. Pi decides to visit the Christian church. He realizes he attends a nominally Christian school, but he has never been inside a church. Even though he says Christianity has "a reputation for few gods and great violence" [p. 64], he is still curious about the faith. Pi notices how peaceful the priests look inside the vestibule. Seeing "neat, plain, simple" priests ready to "listen with love" [p. 65] moves Pi very deeply. Pi eventually gathers the courage to enter the church, where he meets Father Martin. After listening to Father Martin's story about the basis of Christianity, Pi experiences feelings of disbelief and confusion. The story doesn't make sense to him. Pi says it is a "downright weird" tale with a "peculiar psychology." The idea that a God should suffer humiliation and death for His followers confuses Pi, especially when he was raised on stories of all-powerful Hindu gods, whom Pi could not imagine "consenting to be stripped naked, whipped, mocked, dragged through the streets and…crucified" [p. 68]. Father Martin tells Pi that the reason for this suffering and sacrifice is love. Still, Pi is bothered, even angered, by this story, yet he cannot stop thinking about it.)*

4. How does Pi discover Islam, and what does he find so fascinating about the faith? *(About a year after discovering Christianity, Pi explores the Muslim quarter of his hometown. Pi thinks that "Islam [has] a reputation worse than Christianity's—fewer gods, greater violence…" [p. 73], and he is afraid to go near the mosque. Pi enters a small shop near the mosque and meets a baker, who invites Pi in to speak with him. As they are talking, Pi hears a sound ring out from the direction of the mosque and the baker begins the Islamic prayer ritual. Pi finds the ritual "quick, necessary, physical, muttered, striking" [p. 76], and when he finally tries the prayer ritual himself, Pi feels it is a deeply spiritual and humble act. Pi learns about Islam from Satish Kumar, the baker, and sees Islam as "a beautiful religion of brotherhood and devotion" [p. 77].)*

5. Describe the two times Pi "felt God" come close to him. *(One time when cycling back from praying with Mr. Kumar, he stopped at a high point where he could see the ocean. Pi suddenly felt like he was in heaven, even though the place had not changed since he last saw it. Rather, his perspective changed from praying with Mr. Kumar. Everything spoke differently to him. Pi "felt like the centre of a small circle coinciding with the centre of a much larger one" [p. 79]. The second time*

was in Canada, much later in life. Pi was walking in the countryside during the winter when a breeze knocked some snow off a branch, and in the falling, sparkling flakes, Pi saw the image of the Virgin Mary, though not literally. But his vision filled him with both fear and joy.)

6. Discuss the negative effects of Pi's religious diversity. Who confronts Pi about this issue, and what do these people think about his devotions to numerous faiths? *(When people begin to notice that Pi is getting involved with various religions, they began to ask questions, and the matter was "forcefully brought to the attention of [Pi's] bemused parents" [p. 81]. Ravi often makes fun of Pi for his many faiths as well. People glare at him, frighten him, and generally disapprove of his actions. A priest, an imam, and a pandit each go to the zoo to speak to Pi about his faith. As each one states that Pi is a devout follower of one religion, the others scoff and protest. It devolves into a shouting match where each religious leader puts down the other's faith, slandering one another's tenets and history. They each chastise Pi for being a member of more than one faith at a time and demand that he choose one.)*

7. How do Pi's parents react to the religious leaders' demands and to Pi's response? *(At first, Pi's parents are silent. However, when the men force Pi to choose, Pi's father says he does not think what Pi is doing is a crime but also asks Pi to choose. When Pi says, "'All religions are true.' I just want to love God" [p. 87], Pi's father agrees with him. Pi's parents decide that they cannot reprimand Pi for his honest, pure intentions.)*

8. Regarding Christianity and Islam, what two desires does Pi eventually fulfill, and how does he do so? *(Pi approaches his father and asks to be baptized. He also asks for an Islamic prayer rug. His father once again insists that he cannot be both Christian and Muslim because they "have nothing in common" [p. 91]. Pi, his mother, and his father discuss the issue at length. Pi's parents can see him being interested in Christianity, but his interest in Islam is unfathomable to them. Pi's parents try to pass his questions off on each other and wonder why their son cannot have normal interests for a boy his age. After much debate, they buy him a prayer rug and allow him to be baptized.)*

9. Discuss the process Pi's family goes through to sell the zoo and move to Canada. *(Pi's family sells the entire zoo, mostly to American zoos because they are willing to pay more for the animals. The family realizes they sold their zoo at the right time because CITES, the Convention on International Trade in Endangered Species, had just been put into effect, banning the trade of captured wild animals. The money the family makes from the sales is enough to pay for their travel, immigration, and relocation in Canada. Ravi and Pi are not enthusiastic about moving to Canada. The entire process of selling the zoo takes about a year. The family spends a fortune on phone calls and stamps in order to fill out all of the required paperwork. Pi's father works endlessly to organize the animals' transportation, and he makes trades to acquire desirable animals that sell at higher prices. Americans come to visit and purchase many animals. After a year's toil, the family packs their remaining belongings and boards the ship to Canada.)*

10. **Prediction:** The Patel family takes a cargo ship out of India. In what way will this affect the plot as opposed to taking a passenger ship?

Supplementary Activities

1. With a partner or in a group, choose a scene from this section and perform the scene for the class. Be sure to emphasize any deeper meaning or symbolism the scene may hold.

2. Reread the descriptions of the following characters or places: Father Martin, Mr. Kumar (the teacher), Mr. Kumar (the Muslim mystic), the Christian church/vestibule in Munnar, Pi's Toronto home, the mosque, or the two places where Pi felt close to God. Choose one, and find or create photographs, paintings, sketches, or other pieces of art that match the description given to create a class collage.

3. Choose three vocabulary words from this section, and find a synonym or antonym for each. Using these synonyms/antonyms, write a three-sentence synopsis of this section.

Chapters 37–52

Pi wakes up to a strange noise. He goes exploring and discovers that the ship is sinking. Before he can reach his parents, the ship's crew throws Pi into a lifeboat. The ship sinks, and Pi appears to be the only human survivor. Pi finds himself in the lifeboat with a wounded zebra, a hyena, an orang-utan named Orange Juice, and a 450-pound Bengal tiger named Richard Parker. Pi avoids the animals as much as possible by staying on top of the taut tarpaulin that covers half the boat and by hanging off the prow of the boat. Richard Parker remains under the tarpaulin while the hyena eats the zebra and eventually attacks Orange Juice. After a brutal fight, the hyena kills and eats Orange Juice. Pi watches the carnage helplessly, realizing he may be next. The tiger's presence keeps the hyena at the other end of the boat, giving Pi time to investigate the food and supply locker in the bow of the lifeboat, where he finds many useful and lifesaving items.

Vocabulary
dyspeptic
ensconced
flotsam
aversion
dishevelled
remonstrations
empathy
abomination
empirical
supplication
catchment

Discussion Questions

1. Describe Pi's actions on the morning of the ship's sinking, and explain how he survived. *(Pi thinks he hears an explosion and wakes up early in the morning. Although the ship is always noisy, these sounds are unexpected and irregular, waking Pi with a start. Pi gets dressed and tries to wake his brother, without success. Alone, Pi ascends two levels to the desk of the ship where he sees that it is raining. The sea looks rough, and though he feels he is on a great adventure, he soon realizes that the ship is lilting ever so slightly. He returns inside and hears "deep structural groans," but before he can reach his parents, he sees water surging up toward him. Rushing to the deck again, Pi is now fully aware of the danger he is in. Pi hears animals shrieking and sees some escaping onto the deck. Pi runs and finds three crew members who grab him, put a lifejacket on him, and then throw him overboard into a lifeboat below. He lands on the tarpaulin above the boat, and the men shout for him to get into the boat. A zebra then jumps over them and down into the boat, crashing onto a bench. The boat breaks free and drifts away from the sinking ship, making Pi the only human aboard the lifeboat.)*

2. What fears does Pi deal with on the first day, and how is he able to avoid Richard Parker? *(Pi is afraid to be in the water, where he initially goes to avoid Richard Parker. When Pi sees sharks, he climbs aboard a lifebuoy and eventually onto the edge of the lifeboat. Pi sees that Richard Parker is hiding underneath the tarpaulin. Even though he is out of Richard Parker's sight, which is very keen, Pi knows that tigers still have a better sense of smell and better hearing than humans do, so the danger is still very real. Pi fears that the tiger will claw its way through the tarp and attack him, but it never happens, and Pi eventually climbs on top of the tarpaulin. He is relatively safe there, as long as he stays out of Richard Parker's sight, but he keeps himself poised to escape onto the prow or even dive back into the Pacific. Pi knows he will have to deal with "one terror at a time" [p. 134] if he is to survive.)*

3. What does Pi think will happen to him in a few hours? What does Pi think happened to his parents? Do you think these thoughts are helpful or harmful? *(Pi is certain he is not alone and that someone else must have survived. He imagines that alarms are going off in cities all over the world, that pilots are running for their planes, and that submarines are changing course to join the rescue search. Pi is sure a ship will appear to rescue him soon. Pi believes a rescue ship picked up his family from another lifeboat and that they will be reunited soon. Answers will vary. Some will believe that these hopes are foolish and detrimental to Pi's spirit because they are very unlikely to be true. It will be a crushing blow when Pi realizes his family members are dead. Others may think that Pi's hopeful outlook will help him survive.)*

4. From the information Pi presents, describe a hyena's appearance, mannerisms, and eating habits. *(Hyenas are "ugly beyond redemption," with thick necks, high shoulders, and a "shaggy, coarse coat…patched together from the leftovers of creation" [p. 145]. The hyena's coat looks "like the symptoms of a skin disease, a virulent form of mange" [p. 145]. It has a broad, massive head with slack jaws that always hang open. Contrary to popular belief, hyenas are not cowardly, but rather clever. Hyenas hunt and attack in packs. They hunt zebras, gnus, water buffalo, and even young lions or young rhinoceros. A pack of hyenas can gnaw its prey down to the bone, often becoming ill from overeating and sometimes coughing up hairballs. "Its delights are too many to admit to disgust at anything" [p. 146], and it will even eat feces, drink urine, and attack its own young. Hyenas even attack motor vehicles, using their formidable jaws to rip apart the metal.)*

5. How does Pi explain the strange manner in which the hyena and Orange Juice initially act around each other? *(Pi sees Orange Juice sitting with her back to the hyena, ignoring it, and the hyena doesn't attack. He finds this "decidedly baffling." The only conclusion he can come to is because "there are no natural conditions in which a spotted hyena and an orang-utan can meet…there is no way of knowing how they would relate" [p. 153]. Even so, Pi finds this strange because Orange Juice must surely sense that the hyena is a predator, and the hyena must surely see Orange Juice as easy prey, yet "nature forever holds surprises" [p. 154].)*

6. How do Orange Juice and the hyena eventually acknowledge each other, and what is the final result? *(While the hyena continues to eat the zebra alive, Orange Juice becomes riled and stands on her bench, raises her arms, and roars at the hyena. It is "a deep, powerful, huffing roar" [p. 158] which startles both the hyena and Pi. In response, the hyena stands atop the zebra, opens its bloody jaws, and roars back. Both continue to roar, and even the zebra begins to cry out in pain and terror. After a few terrible minutes of screaming, the hyena and Orange Juice back off and return to their positions in the boat. Silence falls on the boat, and Pi sinks into misery as the hyena continues to eat the zebra. The next day, Pi notices the palpable tension between the animals on the lifeboat. Violence breaks out in the afternoon. As the hyena jumps for Orange Juice, she punches him in the head. Her fierce display of defense fills Pi with "love and admiration and fear" [p. 162]. But the moment doesn't last long. The hyena attacks again, and Pi knows that Orange Juice will soon lose the fight. After a brief struggle, the hyena kills Orange Juice with a bite to the throat. Pi knows that he may very well be next.)*

7. What discovery does Pi make when he advances to defend himself from the hyena, and how does it change his perspective about the behavior of the lifeboat's animals? *(When Pi crosses the tarpaulin to defend himself from the hyena, he sees Richard Parker nestled on the floor of the lifeboat. Pi thought the tiger had left the boat and that he only had the hyena to fear. Now he knows a 450-pound Bengal tiger is aboard the boat. Richard Parker's presence explains why Orange Juice kept her back to the hyena rather than facing it, and it explains why the hyena took so long to eat the zebra and attack Orange Juice. A bigger predator was in the boat, but when the tiger made no move to assert his alpha status, the hyena felt it was safe to attack the weaker prey. Now Pi has two predators to fear.)*

8. How did Richard Parker get his name? Do you find the name appropriate? *(The tiger is named Richard Parker "because of a clerical error" [p. 166]. A hunter named Richard Parker was once hired to find a panther terrorizing the Khulna district of Bangladesh. When the hunter found a tiger instead, he shot it with a dart gun to remove the potential threat to human life. The female tiger's cub was hiding in the bushes, meowing with fear. The hunter named the baby cub "Thirsty," but the newspapers got it backward. Since then, people referred to the tiger as Richard Parker and the hunter as Thirsty. Answers will vary. Some students may find Richard Parker's name absurdly fitting, while others may find the name "Thirsty" more appropriate, if not ironic, especially for a tiger lost at sea where there is no potable drinking water.)*

9. How does Richard Parker's presence save Pi's life? *(Once Pi discovers the tiger is indeed still aboard the lifeboat, he knows his life is over. Since nothing worse can happen but death, Pi decides to have a drink before he dies. His impending death makes all other fears, such as the lack of water, feel like nothing at all. By prompting Pi to search for water, Richard Parker saves Pi's life because Pi discovers that the lifeboat has a secret cache of supplies, including food, water, and tools to help castaways survive. Richard Parker's presence also protects Pi from the hyena. The hyena watches Pi from the other end of the boat, and Pi does not fear the animal any longer. Pi says, "To be afraid of [that] ridiculous dog when there was a tiger about was like being afraid of splinters when trees are falling down" [p. 171].)*

10. **Prediction:** Of the supplies Pi finds in the lifeboat, which do you think will be most beneficial to his survival? Why?

Supplementary Activities

1. Review Pi's complete list of supplies, and then choose only five items from that list to use for your own "Pacific Survival Kit." As a class, read your choices aloud and discuss the pros and cons of each. Then compile a "Top Ten List" of Pi's most useful supplies.

2. Complete the Sociogram on page 33 of this guide, which explores the relationships between the survivors on the lifeboat.

3. Conduct Internet research to find out the significance of the name "Richard Parker." Why did Martel choose this name for the tiger? What other famous uses of the name "Richard Parker" did you find, and how are they related?

Chapters 53–65

Pi is wracked by thoughts of a slow, agonizing death from thirst and hunger or a quick one from being attacked by Richard Parker or the hyena, but a voice inside tells him to hold out and trust in God. Pi builds a small raft to keep away from the lifeboat just as Richard Parker finally attacks the hyena. With his raft, Pi is able to keep a good distance between him and the lifeboat. Pi struggles with various plans of action, but none seem feasible. As Pi learns to use his survival tools to acquire food and water, he realizes that the only way he will survive in the long-term is to train Richard Parker into thinking Pi is the alpha animal. Pi passes the time praying, gathering what food and water he can, and learning to cope with Richard Parker's constant presence.

Vocabulary
lucidity
lithesome
attrition
mantra
unerring
brackish
galleon
evanescent
sentient
sanguinary
mutinous

Discussion Questions

1. How does Pi react to the threat Richard Parker poses? How do the two predators react to one another, and how does Pi escape them? *(Pi knows very well that Richard Parker could kill him at any moment, and the tension between the tiger and the hyena is escalating. Pi knows the two predators will soon attack one another, and eventually, him. Pi knows that "to leave the lifeboat [means] certain death" [p. 185], but the alternative is even more frightening. Pi envisions Richard Parker mauling him, and immobilizing fear overcomes him. Just as Pi gives up, an inner voice refuses to accept defeat. He knows he must save himself, if only for the short-term. Pi hastily decides to build a lifeboat out of lifejackets and floatable oars as the two beasts begin to snarl at one another. Just as he finishes a makeshift raft, Richard Parker attacks the hyena. The sight of Richard Parker mauling the hyena is one that Pi will never forget. When it is over, Richard Parker turns to Pi and snarls. At that moment, a rat appears. Pi snatches it up and throws the rat toward Richard Parker. Satisfied with the small morsel of food, Richard Parker turns to the dead hyena. Pi then jumps into his lifeboat where he is temporarily safe.)*

2. How is Pi able to supply enough water for himself and Richard Parker? *(Pi has cans of water in the lifeboat, but he knows that will not be enough. He also has rain catchers that look like upside-down umbrellas with tubes and plastic bags attached, which he uses during storms. He drinks even if he isn't thirsty so no water goes to waste. Pi also uses solar stills, which create fresh water from sea water by gathering condensation inside inflatable cones. The sun beats down on the sea, and drinkable water rises up inside the cone and is gathered into bags. Using these, Pi is able to secure enough drinking water for himself and for Richard Parker even if it doesn't rain for a long time.)*

3. What plans does Pi consider in order to deal with Richard Parker, and what is wrong with each of them? How does he come up with his final solution? Which plan do you think is best, and why? *(The first plan is to push the tiger off the lifeboat. However, forcibly moving a 450-pound tiger is impossible. Also, even if Pi accomplished this feat, Richard Parker [being an excellent swimmer] would probably just climb right back on. The second plan is to kill Richard Parker with morphine from the survival kit, but Pi thinks even all six syringes might not be enough to kill the tiger. The third plan is to attack Richard Parker with all available weaponry. Pi realizes this is foolhardy, as he could never kill the tiger before getting mauled himself. Pi's fourth plan, to choke Richard Parker with a rope, is too complicated and dangerous. Pi considers poisoning him, setting him on fire, and electrocuting him, but he has no feasible way of doing this. Pi then decides to "Wage a War of Attrition" [p. 200] against Richard Parker. Although this plan seems initially to be the best, Pi soon realizes that Richard Parker would easily outlast him and eventually swim out to Pi's raft and eat him long before starvation hit. The only other alternative is finding a way to coexist with Richard Parker. A part of Pi doesn't want Richard Parker to die because then Pi will be alone. He needs the distraction of the tiger in order to survive. Pi decides to tame Richard Parker. He has the tools, time, and will to do it and no alternative. Answers will vary, but most students will see the folly of Pi's first six plans and agree that training Richard Parker is his best chance for survival.)*

4. Of all the tips in the survival guide, which do you think may be most useful to Pi, and why? Which tip is missing, according to Pi? *(Answers will vary. Some of the more useful tips may be the advice about which sea creatures are edible, tips on navigation, health tips about conserving energy, how to tell deep water from shallow water, or the suggestion to keep spirits high in spite of the circumstances. All are useful to some degree. The tip missing is "the establishing of alpha-omega relationships with major lifeboat pests" [p. 211].)*

5. After reading the survival guide, what things does Pi decide he must do to survive? Explain how each action is necessary to Pi's survival. *(First, Pi knows he must devise a plan to train Richard Parker so he believes Pi is the "top tiger" and that Pi's territory is the tarpaulin and bow of the boat. Pi must systematically teach Richard Parker that Pi is the dominant being on the boat if they are to live peaceably with one another. Without Pi, Richard Parker will die, and Pi wants to keep Richard Parker alive for companionship. Therefore, Pi must train the tiger. Second, Pi must start fishing because Richard Parker will soon devour the rest of the dead animals on the lifeboat, leaving him with no food. Third, Pi must make a shelter for himself because the exposure could result in exhaustion and a quick death. Fourth, Pi must tie the raft to the lifeboat to ensure he will not lose the lifeboat and the supplies it holds. He must also improve the raft so it is habitable. Pi must stay dry or else he will become wrinkled, swollen, and eventually get sick and die. Fifth, Pi must stop hoping that a ship will rescue him. The hope of rescue kept him alive in his early days at sea, but he now knows that "a castaway's worst mistake is to hope too much and do too little" [p. 212]. Despite his overwhelming loneliness, Pi must start paying attention to the opportunities around him and take action.)*

6. Why is the lifeboat the perfect place to train Richard Parker? *(Pi realizes that the lifeboat resembles a zoo enclosure. Richard Parker has a place to sleep and rest, a food stash, a lookout, a watering hole, and is relatively content, all things considered. Pi had earlier observed that the ocean is the "perfect circus ring, inescapably round, without a single corner for [Richard Parker] to hide in" [p. 207], and Pi has the whistle for a whip, the ocean for rewards [fish], and all the time in the world. There will be no distractions to Pi's tiger training.)*

7. What opportunities for survival does the ocean offer, and how does Pi use those opportunities? *(Pi discovers that "the sea is a city…bustling with submarine traffic" [p. 221]. Fish swim through the sea below him, leaving long, glowing trails of shimmering light. Pi first thought that the Pacific was "a sparsely inhabited waste of water" [p. 222] but learns that the ocean offers plenty of food if he can learn to fish. His first attempts fail when he uses bits of leather from his shoe as bait. Then the ocean seems to offer him food when flying fish swarm the lifeboat. Pi is able to capture some, but Richard Parker catches more. Using pieces of the flying fish as bait, Pi is able to catch one of the monstrously huge dorados, satisfying Richard Parker's appetite. The process of fishing takes up a lot of Pi's time, but "the feeling of busyness was profoundly satisfying" [p. 235]. Pi also realizes that he must start hunting for turtles, a suggestion offered by the lifeboat's survival guide.)*

8. Describe a typical day for Pi. What activities take up the majority of his time? Why does he establish a routine? *(Pi wakes, prays, feeds Richard Parker, inspects the raft and lifeboat, tends the solar stills, eats and inspects his food, fishes, and prays again before lunch. After lunch, he rests, writes in his journal, inspects sores, observes Richard Parker, and then prays again. As the evening falls, Pi fishes again, cures strips of drying flesh, prepares dinner for Richard Parker, inspects the raft's ropes again, collects water from the solar stills, stores food and equipment, prepares for sleep, and prays again before closing his eyes. Pi works on training Richard Parker, but not daily. He "spaces out" Richard Parker's lessons. Answers will vary, but prayer, hunting and searching for food, and inspecting equipment seems to take up most of Pi's time. Pi's routine helps his mind stay busy so he doesn't drive himself insane with worry, fear, or regret.)*

9. How does Pi deal with the passage of time? *(Answers will vary. Pi drifts for 227 days, unable to navigate, and he survives by forgetting "the very notion of time" [p. 242]. He does not count the days, weeks, or months. His memory has many holes because of the long passages of time during which little happens. He remembers random things like the smell of spent hand-flare shells, praying, and killing turtles, but his memories are jumbled.)*

10. **Prediction:** How, if ever, will Pi be rescued?

Supplementary Activities

1. Research the amount of food an average tiger would eat in a week. Considering the average weight of a dorado, is it possible for Pi to catch enough fish to feed Richard Parker? Write a brief essay explaining your opinion.

2. Using a medium of your choice, create an original artistic rendition of the ocean's "city" and "highway" system to display for the class.

3. Divide into groups of two or three students, and write a condensed "High School Survival Guide." Be sure to include tips for getting through an average day, semester, and year of high school, written in the same manner as the survival tips found on pages 209–211 of the novel.

Chapters 66–86

Pi becomes a better fisherman, even feasting upon turtles, but his other supplies in the boat run low. Pi has trouble sleeping and occasionally thinks he sees lights in the distance, but he is unable to hail them with his flares. Pi continues Richard Parker's training. The training is dangerous, and Pi uses turtle shells as shields, though he loses the first four when Richard Parker knocks him off the boat and into the water. He dreams of books and continues to practice religious rituals to pass the time and build up his spiritual fortitude, but as food runs low, life becomes a difficult series of opposites. He is either too hot or too cold, too full or hungry, bored or terrified. A vicious storm destroys Pi's small raft, but the two castaways survive with the rest of their supplies. Whales, dolphins, and birds approach their boat, but there is still no sign of land.

Vocabulary
tilaks
translucent
forbearance
misconstrue
malaise
pendulum
gregarious
hillocks
archipelago
heinous
exalted

Discussion Questions

1. While hunting, Pi says he "descended to a level of savagery [he] never imagined possible" (p. 249). What does he mean by this? *(While there are periods of starvation, there are also bouts of plenty when Pi has more food than he needs. During those times, he catches so many fish that his body glitters with their scales. He becomes adept at killing turtles, which is an exhausting but jubilant task. Pi is thankful for the meat and thinks wryly about how he used to be a strict vegetarian. He now eats as an animal would, "noisy, frantic, unchewing" [p. 284]. He kills for food, and this makes him feel more savage than he ever imagined he could.)*

2. How does Pi's sleeping pattern change, and why? *(Unlike Richard Parker, who sleeps all the time, Pi only sleeps for short intervals. For the sake of his health, he spends a lot of time resting, but sleep eludes him. It isn't the motion of the waves that keeps Pi awake, but rather the anxiety and apprehension that he feels. Reasons for Pi's anxiety will vary, but seeing how he lives in a constant, stressful state of near-starvation, it is no wonder that Pi cannot sleep.)*

3. Explain Pi's detailed plan for training Richard Parker. What is the most dangerous aspect of this plan? *(1. Wait for a day when the waves are small but regular. 2. Stream the sea anchor full out to make the lifeboat stable and comfortable. Also, create some means of bodily protection. 3. Provoke the animal by noisily intruding into the neutral zone. Make a consistent, recognizable noise and stare into its eyes, but do not intrude upon its territory. 4. As the animal is roused, back off slowly while making noise, but do not break eye contact. Make the animal advance. 5. Once the animal steps into your territory, blow the whistle at full blast and trip the sea anchor, which will make the lifeboat rock violently, making the animal sick. This must be done immediately. 6. Keep blowing the whistle and help rock the lifeboat, but do not capsize the ship. 7. Keep doing this until the animal is on the bottom of the boat, seasick and trembling. If you get sick too, puke on the edge of your territory. 8. You can stop when the animal is "good and sick" because the sickness will come on quickly but take longer to go away. Retreat and leave the animal in peace. The animal must be allowed to recover before repeating these steps. 9. "Treatment should be repeated until association in the animal's mind between the sound of the whistle and the feeling of...nausea is fixed and totally unambiguous" [p. 259]. Once you reach this level of training, use the whistle sparingly. Answers will vary. One could fall overboard when trying to rock the boat, or the animal may simply attack and kill before nausea can take effect. The entire practice is dangerous, but vital.)*

4. What happens when Pi attempts to put his plan into action, and why does Pi believe Richard Parker does not kill him? *(The first time Pi advances, the tiger swipes at the boy with his paw, violently knocking him overboard. Pi loses his turtle shell shield when he falls into the sea, and loses the next three the same way. On Pi's fifth attempt, the plan works, and Richard Parker never knocks Pi overboard again. Even though Richard Parker swipes at Pi and growls, Pi doesn't believe the tiger actually wants to attack him. He knows tigers do not usually resort to violence to settle a grudge, and Pi notices Richard Parker often gives warnings before he attacks. Pi learns to read the warnings and in this way avoids injury. Another part of Pi also likely hopes that Richard Parker has a fondness for him, something beyond respect and need.)*

5. When Pi begins to ration food, to what extent does he go to fulfill his cravings? *(Pi is in a constant state of hunger when he rations his biscuits and water, and he dreams of massive, endless meals. "Every meal was simply perfect—only just beyond the reach of [his] hands" [p. 267]. Pi starts to eat any and every part of the fish and turtles he catches, even the fluid from the eyes or food inside a turtle's stomach. Pi nearly eats Richard Parker's feces but quickly realizes he can't bring himself to do it.)*

6. What does Pi mean when he says, "To be a castaway is to be a point perpetually at the centre of a circle" (p. 272)? *(A castaway in the ocean is surrounded by the same view all the time, a circle of water that doesn't seem to end, unchanging from day to day. "...the geometry never changes. Your gaze is always a radius" [p. 272]. The sun and moon chase each other, and you are caught in the middle of that circular cycle as well. There are no edges, no corners, nothing to hold onto but yourself—a tiny dot in the middle of nothing.)*

7. What does Pi mean when he says, "to be a castaway is to be caught up in grim and exhausting opposites" (p. 273)? *(Everything comes in extremes. Pi is either too hot in the daytime or too cold at night. He is either starving or has too much food to cure and keep. When it is hot he wants to be wet to cool down, and when it rains he wants nothing more than to be warm and dry. When the sea is flat, he wants it to stir, and when it rolls in great hills of water, he wants it to be still. "The worst pair of opposites is boredom and terror" [p. 274]. When the hours last forever, Pi longs for something, anything, to happen. When something does happen, it is usually something terrifying, which makes Pi crave peace once again. There is never a happy middle ground.)*

8. How does Pi know he has finally dominated Richard Parker? *(In a hail of flying fish, Pi catches a giant dorado. Pi catches the fish more with luck than skill. During the barrage of flying fish, the dorado slams into the gunnel and falls into the water, dead. Pi scoops the fish up, and then Richard Parker turns his head toward Pi. The tiger, like Pi, is starving and wants the fish. Pi senses the tiger is about to attack. Though Pi is in a weakened state, he stares Richard Parker down, his eyes wide and defiant, until Richard Parker licks his nose, groans, and turns away. In that moment, Pi knows he has trained the tiger and that he, Pi, is the master.)*

9. What kinds of visitors do Pi and Richard Parker receive? Why are the birds in particular so disappointing to Pi? *(A whale rises to the surface beside the lifeboat and stares at Pi before slipping back into the water. Pi is afraid the whale might overturn the lifeboat, but it never does. Dolphins are also "fairly regular visitors," and one group stays with them for a whole day and night. Pi also sees six birds in total. He thinks each is an angel announcing nearby land. None of them ever do. Each time he sees a bird, Pi is disappointed that there is no land in sight.)*

10. What happens when Pi finally sees a ship? *(Pi is ecstatic. As the tanker approaches, Pi thinks again of his parents, hoping they are alive. Then Pi realizes with horror that the ship is not just heading their way, but is bearing down right on top of them with no sign of slowing down. Richard Parker begins to bark at the ship, and the massive oil tanker slides by them, just missing the lifeboat. It goes by for what seems like a mile. Pi fires off a rocket flare, but he aims it poorly. The flare bounces off the hull and lands in the water. Pi blows his whistle and shouts, but the ship doesn't stop. It is too big, too loud, and the crew most likely is not paying attention. The ship is a speck on the horizon in 20 minutes, and Pi sinks into despair. He shouts a promise to Richard Parker that he will save them somehow.)*

Supplementary Activities

1. Pi says that the life of a castaway is one of opposites. Look at your own life, and write an essay about the opposites you see. Write at least three sets of extreme opposites, and explain them in the same manner Pi explains his.

2. Pi says his greatest wish, aside from salvation, is to have a book. If you were lost at sea, what book would you choose to have with you? As a class, share your choices to make a comprehensive list. Which choice is the most surprising? the most popular?

Chapters 87–93

Pi continues to drift across the Pacific, slowly succumbing to exposure, hunger, and thirst. He believes he and Richard Parker are close to death. Pi goes blind and finally resigns himself to death. Through his blindness he hears a voice, which he thinks is Richard Parker's. He joyfully realizes the voice is another human, a Frenchman who says he is also blind and drifting in a lifeboat. As the two boats meet, the Frenchman tries to kill Pi. Richard Parker attacks the Frenchman, and even though Pi almost died, he is horrified at the loss of another human life. To his relief, Pi regains his vision shortly after the encounter with the Frenchman. Pi and Richard Parker discover an island made entirely of strange, tube-like algae. The algae are edible, and the island on which they grow is full of meerkats and strange pools of freshwater where dead fish appear. Pi and Richard Parker eat their fill and return to the boat at night. After further exploration, Pi finds that the algae are carnivorous. Pi even finds teeth, a sign that other humans once found the same island but were consumed by the algae. Pi and Richard Parker reluctantly return to the Pacific. Pi turns his attention to God and continues his journey.

Vocabulary

emaciated
infernal
sacrilegious
amoral
famishing
eviscerated
commensal
vagaries
symbiotic
conjecture
deprivation
bereft

Discussion Questions

1. What is one of Pi's favorite methods of escape? Why do you think he enjoys it, and how do you feel about this method? *(Pi cuts off a piece of his blanket and uses it to asphyxiate himself into a semi-conscious state by laying it across his face. He calls it his "dream rag." While unconscious, Pi is "visited by the most extraordinary dreams, trances, visions, thoughts, sensations, [and] remembrances" [p. 299] which take up vast amounts of idle time. By passing time in a dream state, Pi is able to remove himself from his helpless situation and occupy his mind. Answers will vary. Some students will find this method dangerous and unhealthy, both physically and mentally. Others may argue that Pi needs to do something to distance his mind from his horrible situation.)*

2. Why does Pi no longer feel that he can take care of Richard Parker? Why does Richard Parker's death sadden him more than his own? *(Richard Parker and Pi are both going blind. After realizing this, Pi becomes "weakly frantic," realizing he cannot hunt for food or collect water if he cannot see. Pi knows this means both he and Richard Parker have a very short time to live. As a zookeeper's son, Pi feels like a failure for not being able to keep such a magnificent animal alive. Also, since Richard Parker was the one thing keeping Pi alive, Pi knows that Richard Parker's death only makes Pi's death more imminent.)*

3. Discuss Pi's initial feelings about the voice he hears. What does Pi discuss with the voice, and to whom does Pi think the voice belongs? What happens when Pi meets the owner of the voice? *(The voice surprises Pi and makes him think he has gone crazy, his mind playing tricks on him. An absurd conversation about "figments" and "figs" soon begins, followed by a conversation about foods the two crave. While all of the foods that Pi wants are vegetarian dishes, the other speaker craves meat. This makes Pi think that Richard Parker, "the carnivorous rascal" [p. 310], is somehow speaking to him. When Pi notices a French accent, he realizes it is not his imagination or Richard Parker, but another human being. They discuss lack of food, their blindness, and their predicament. The Frenchman rows over to Pi's lifeboat, and Pi senses the man right in front of him. As Pi realizes he should tell this new friend about the tiger, the Frenchman attempts to strangle Pi, presumably so he can cannibalize Pi's dead body. As Pi begs for mercy, Richard Parker attacks and kills the Frenchman.)*

4. Why do you think Pi feels no joy when Richard Parker rescues him from the murderous hands of the Frenchman? *(Answers will vary. On one hand, Pi is grateful that Richard Parker saved his life, but he did it "at the expense of taking one" [p. 321]. Even as the Frenchman is strangling Pi, Pi still tries to warn the man that a tiger is aboard, calling him "brother" as he pleads for the man to be careful. Pi is such a peaceful person and is so desperate to be around another human that the loss of another's life, even a murderer's life, is devastating to him.)*

5. What "exceptional botanical discovery" does Pi make, and how does he initially react to this discovery? How does this discovery improve Pi's life? *(Pi recovers his sight just in time to discover a floating mass of vegetation, an island made of algae and trees but no soil. At first, he thinks it is an illusion, even when he gets close to the island. As the survival book tells him, "...a foot is the only good judge of land..." [p. 324], so Pi steps onto the vegetation. It is flexible but solid, and the realization that he has actually found land shocks Pi. He is not used to walking and almost faints as he tries to stay on his feet. The excitement is almost too much for him. Answers will vary. The discovery is a huge boost to Pi's spirit, and the island provides him with limitless amounts of food [the meerkats, dead fish, and sweet-tasting algae] and fresh water. Exploring the island also gives Pi something to do as his body and mind grow strong from the newfound stimulation and nutrition.)*

6. What happens on the island at night, and why does Pi decide to leave? Would you have stayed on the island? Why or why not? *(At night, all the meerkats run for shelter in branches of the trees, and even Richard Parker refuses to sleep on the algae floor of the island. The algae tubes seem to bother his paws, and he returns to the boat each night. The fish in the pools of fresh water dissolve and disappear. Pi finds this strange and sinister. Pi finds a tree that appears to bear fruit, and as Pi unpeels the fruit, he finds human teeth. When Pi walks on the algae at night, his feet burn, and then it dawns on him: the algae island is carnivorous. The island dissolves and eats the fish in the pools of water, and the island digested whatever human lived on the island prior to Pi's landing. Pi realizes there is no feasible way to live on the carnivorous island. He reasons that he would rather perish while searching for civilization than face the monstrous fate the island poses. Answers will vary. Most students will understand the fear that would accompany living on the island and agree that leaving is the best idea. Others may think that the island provides everything Pi needs and that there are ways to live around the island's carnivorous nature.)*

7. How does Pi prepare for his departure, and why does he take Richard Parker, a dangerous animal, with him? *(Pi fills every container he can find with fresh water and drinks as much water as he can. He eats algae all day long and kills as many meerkats as he can fit on the boat. He collects dead fish from the ponds. He also hacks off a large chunk of algae and ties it to the boat with rope. Pi takes Richard Parker because "to leave him would mean to kill him" [p. 357]. Richard Parker is his only companion, and Pi has come to appreciate him. He knows the tiger would not survive the first night and he could never live with the guilt of leaving Richard Parker.)*

8. Which threat do you think is the most frightening, the island or the Frenchman? Why? *(Answers will vary. Those who choose the Frenchman may comment on his cannibalistic nature and the fact that he tried to trick Pi into thinking he was a friend. The threat posed by the Frenchman was imminent and violent, and Pi undoubtedly would have been killed if Richard Parker hadn't been present. Those who choose the island may comment that while the threat of death on the island is much less imminent, staying there would be living in a constant state of fear. While Pi could bargain and interact with a human such as the Frenchman, the island would have no mercy or reason for killing its victims.)*

9. **Prediction:** How do you think people will react to Pi's botanical discovery if he ever reaches civilization?

Supplementary Activities

1. Rewrite Pi's "message in a bottle" (p. 300) using at least four vocabulary words from this section.

2. Research carnivorous plants. Choose one, and create a unique poster displaying facts about the plant's structure, discovery, eating habits, habitat, location in the world, and any other pertinent information.

Chapters 94–100

Pi lands in Mexico, and Richard Parker escapes to the jungle without any sort of goodbye, which breaks Pi's heart. The Mexicans who find him and treat him in the hospital are kind and generous, and Pi receives two visitors from the Japanese Ministry of Transport. They ask Pi to explain his story and they question every suspicious detail, equally impressed and confounded by Pi's story, but they are not convinced he is telling the truth. When Pi tells them a different version of the tale, where there are no animals who survive, but people, the two men are shocked. The tale is similar to the original tale, but instead of a hyena, zebra, orang-utan, and tiger, there is the Frenchman, a Chinese sailor, Pi's mother, and Pi. The second tale is so shocking and brutal, where humans are killing and eating each other rather than animals, that the two men prefer to believe the first tale where Richard Parker and Pi survive together, leaving the reader to wonder which tale is true.

Vocabulary

surreptitiously
pliable
ruminants
feral
scimitars
factuality
reprieve
bestial
impressionistic
unparalleled

Discussion Questions

1. Where does Pi eventually land, and why does he cry when he arrives? *(Pi eventually lands on a rural beachfront in Mexico, and locals soon find him. Richard Parker, however, jumps off the boat and disappears into the jungle. Pi begins to weep like a child, not so much because he is overcome by surviving his ordeal or because he is around humans again, but because Richard Parker left him without saying goodbye. Pi feels as though the tiger simply abandoned him, and after all the two have been through together, knowing he will never see Richard Parker again breaks Pi's heart. As Pi says, "What a terrible thing it is to botch a farewell" [p. 360]. He wishes he had had a chance to thank Richard Parker for saving his life, not just by killing the other predators aboard the boat and killing the cannibalistic Frenchman, but by becoming Pi's friend and companion when he needed it most.)*

2. Who pays Pi a visit while he is recovering in the hospital, and what is the intent of this visit? *(Mr. Tomohiro Okamoto and Mr. Atsuro Chiba of the Maritime Department in the Japanese Ministry of Transport arrive in Tomatlán to speak to Pi. They are required to file a report about the ship that sank since it was a Japanese-owned vessel and Pi is the only survivor. They hope to find clues that might lead to discovering the cause of the ship's sinking.)*

3. Why don't Mr. Okamoto and Mr. Chiba believe Pi's first story, and how does Pi counter each of their questions? Do you feel the two men make a compelling argument discounting Pi's story? Why or why not? *(The men do not believe the story because it contains too many unlikely scenarios, which they elucidate one by one. They point out that bananas do not float, which would disprove how Orange Juice made it to the lifeboat. Pi counters their claim by having them float bananas in the sink of his room. Then the men say that some elements of Pi's tale seem like complete fantasy, such as the carnivorous trees, the fish-eating algae that produce fresh water, and the tree-dwelling and aquatic rodents. Pi says it is easy to discount anything you have never seen with your own eyes, using science as an example. The men also find the idea of living with a tiger rather unbelievable, especially since there is no trace of Richard Parker. Pi says animals like tigers naturally try to avoid all human contact, so he is not surprised they have not yet sighted Richard Parker. The two men find Pi and the Frenchman's chance meeting very unlikely. Pi agrees but compares the scenario to a lottery win, which is also unlikely but happens sometimes. The men say the bones aboard the lifeboat do not belong to meerkats, but Pi insists that they do. Answers will vary. Some students will say that the two men point out obvious flaws in Pi's story that anyone*

would question, especially the lack of evidence that Richard Parker was ever present or still lives in the Mexican jungle. Other students may say that the two men are close-minded to refuse to believe a miraculous story simply on the basis that it is "illogical" or has never happened before.)

4. Discuss the role food plays in the interview, and explain Pi's seemingly strange actions when food is offered. *(Throughout the interview, the two Japanese men offer Pi food, mainly to be polite but also to keep him interested in their questions. Once they offer food, Pi begins to ask for more and more. Throughout the course of their interview, he procures cookies, all of the food in the two men's lunches, a chocolate bar, and even lets the men borrow his bananas, only to take them back. Pi hoards the food under his sheet. He offers one of the men a cookie at one point but keeps the rest. What seems humorous at first quickly begins adding up from a psychological standpoint. Pi was at sea for many months, and hoarding food comes naturally to him now. Having "reserves" of food after starving for so long probably makes him feel safe and prepared. Despite the fact that there is an abundance of food now that Pi is back in civilization, he cannot break his habit of saving food.)*

5. Why does Pi offer the men a second story? How is the second story similar to and different from the first? *(Mr. Okamoto says he does not want a story with "invention," only "straight facts." Pi questions their definition of "story" since he sees any story as an invention, whether it is based on true events or not. However, Pi agrees to tell the men a story that will not surprise them and will conform to what they already know about the world. Unlike his first story, Pi's new story involves his mother, an injured Chinese sailor, and the French cook. Aside from the total absence of animals, the two stories are very similar. Each person in Pi's second story seems to bear resemblance to an animal from Pi's first story. The cook [the hyena] was "a disgusting man" who ate anything and was very cruel to everyone else aboard. The Chinese sailor [the zebra] suffered from a broken leg. He could not communicate with the others, and Pi [the tiger] and his mother [the orang-utan] tried to comfort him. The cook eats much of the rations aboard the boat and eventually cannibalizes the sailor. Just as Orange Juice pummeled the hyena, Pi's mother slaps the cook. The tension between the two adults grows. In a wild act, the cook kills Pi's mother. Finally, Pi kills the cook. The actions aboard the boat in the second story exactly mirror the actions in the first story. In each story, Pi is left with a feeling of regret—in the first it is due to lack of closure with Richard Parker, and in the second it is due to letting the evil in his nature engulf him and allow him to cannibalize the cook.)*

6. How do Mr. Okamoto and Mr. Chiba react to Pi's second story, and why do you think they feel this way? *(They see that the two stories match, but they think the second tale is horrific. Since neither story explains how the Tsimtsum sank, Pi is curious about which story the men would prefer to believe. The men admit that they prefer the story with the animals and even tell each other that they must beware of Richard Parker as they drive home. Answers will vary. The human misery in the second story is overwhelmingly depressing, and while the tale is realistic, no humans want to imagine such brutal carnage committed by others of their species. The tale with the animals is much more palatable, fanciful, and interesting, and to a certain degree, it is also believable, especially in the way Pi relates the tale.)*

7. Why does Pi offer the little information he knows about the sinking ship and its crew? *(Pi knows very little about how or why the ship sank, but he seems to want to help the two men make their report. Although he has little technical knowledge of boats, he gives the men information on the weather, unusual sounds he heard, etc. Pi does express his opinion on the quality of the ship, which he calls "a dingy, third-rate rustbucket" [p. 393], and sullen, unfriendly crew, most likely to hint that a drunken crew member could have been responsible for the ship's sinking and for letting the animals loose.)*

8. Which story do you prefer, and why? *(Answers will vary. Students who think creatively and imaginatively will most likely believe the first story. Believing this story requires readers to imagine something outside the realm of reality, to push the limits of possibility, and to believe in things like faith and spirituality that cannot be seen or touched. Students whose thinking is grounded in logic and precision will most likely believe the second story, because although it is gruesome, it does not require readers or listeners to look beyond their existing knowledge of the world. These students might assume that Pi concocted the first story to ease the trauma of what actually happened and that Pi used what was accessible and familiar to him to do so—his supreme knowledge of animals. Ultimately, the author leaves it to readers to answer this question for themselves.)*

Supplementary Activities

1. After Richard Parker escapes into the Jungle, Pi proclaims, "What a terrible thing it is to botch a farewell" (p. 360). Do you think it is worse to botch a first impression or a farewell? Explain your opinion in a one- to two-page essay, using real-life examples where possible.

2. Select four people from your life, and choose an animal that adequately represents each person. Explain your choices in a short paragraph. Be sure to compare personality traits between the person and his or her corresponding animal and show logical reasoning for your selections.

3. Using the Thought Bubble on page 34 of this guide, write what you think Pi is thinking when Mr. Okamoto and Mr. Chiba tell him that they want a tale without invention.

Post-reading Discussion Questions

1. What purpose do faith and religion serve in *Life of Pi*? *(Answers will vary, but religion and faith play huge roles in both the novel and in Pi's life and survival. As a child, Pi is extremely interested in different kinds of faith, believing that "all religions are true" [p. 87]. Though his parents raise him as a Hindu, Pi learns about Christianity and Islam, becoming members of each faith. This gets him into trouble with each group. Church leaders confront him and force him to choose one. When he says that he just wants to love God, they cannot deny him the ability or right to practice any faith he deems worthy. This diverse faith and powerful desire to love God shows a strong will and spirit, perhaps stronger than anyone who follows a single faith. This strength serves Pi well when he is adrift in his lifeboat. While he succumbs to deep regret, angst, suffering, and depression, his love for God keeps him strong enough to persevere. Even with his family gone, and even when he resolves to die, something always happens that reignites Pi's will to survive and give thanks to the God he loves. Pi says that he turns to God time and again. Religion and faith play a large role in Pi's life as an adult as well, as illustrated by the narrator. His house is a temple to his many religious faiths and beliefs, indicating one thing: Pi is sure his life is guided by divine benevolence. A link may also be drawn between Pi's different versions of the story and each religion he practices.)*

2. How does Pi's childhood prepare him for his time spent as a castaway? How does it hurt him? *(Answers will vary, but Pi's childhood seems to help him in three main ways. The first is that Pi learns to swim when many other people turn up their noses at such an activity. This skill becomes vital to Pi when the Tsimtsum sinks and he is knocked overboard. It also helps him lose his fear of water, something he may have struggled with had he not learned to swim. Pi also grows up in a zoo, learning all about animals, their habits, and how to train them. His animal knowledge is extensive for a young boy, and it all comes in very handy when Pi finds himself stranded with the numerous animals in the lifeboat, and even more so when he must train Richard Parker. Finally, Pi's religious studies fortify his spirit and will, making him resilient in the face of adversity. Though Pi does resign himself to death at one point, he likely lasts much longer than someone who practiced no faith would have. His childhood hurts him in some ways. Being a strict vegetarian and pacifist as a child, Pi is initially reluctant to eat any meat or to kill, which hinders his ability to eat and stay strong early on. However, Pi eventually gives in, knowing he must do anything in his power to survive.)*

3. What is an "unreliable narrator," and do you think Pi falls into this category? Why or why not? *(An unreliable narrator is a narrator that tells a story that is discovered later not to be entirely true, to omit certain events and times, or to be a distorted version of the truth. This may be because the narrator is psychologically unstable, has a strong or selfish bias, lacks a comprehensive understanding of what is happening, or is trying to deceive the reader. The reader usually discovers this during a twisted ending, when the author casts doubt upon the reality readers grew to believe. One famous example of this is the narrator in Agatha Christie's* The Murder of Roger Ackroyd, *where the narrator is the murderer, but the reader does not realize this until the end. Answers will vary about Pi. Pi could potentially fall into this category because of the traumatic experiences he witnesses when the ship sinks. If the second story he tells is true, then witnessing his mother's murder and killing the cook in turn creates a psychological breakdown where his mind creates a new story to cope with the horrific situation, thus making most of the novel a complete fabrication and Pi an unreliable narrator. He seems to be a stable, reliable person later in life, but whether or not the tiger story is true is left up to the reader.)*

4. What symbolic meaning may Martel intend for Richard Parker? *(Answers will vary. In the first story, Richard Parker may symbolize the dangers of the wild and Pi's struggle to overcome the elements. If Pi can train Richard Parker [the open sea], he can survive. If he cannot train the tiger, the elements will kill him. In the second story, Pi is obviously Richard Parker. The tiger represents the animal instincts deep inside Pi's psyche. After those instincts manifest themselves with lethal results, Pi knows he must train his instincts and use them to his advantage. While doing this, he cannot allow his brute instincts to overtake his ideals and pacifist beliefs. When Pi reaches Mexico, the animal killer within disappears, and Pi returns to his peaceful self since he no longer needs to survive in the wild.)*

5. Are there any villains in this novel? If so, who (or what) and why? *(Answers will vary. Some will classify the French cook as a villain because he tries to kill Pi in one story and succeeds in killing Pi's mother in the other. Even though the cook likely killed solely for survival, the fact that he resorted to treachery and murder pushes him into the realm of evil. Some may say that Richard Parker is a villain, as he poses a deadly threat to Pi, but this response is much less likely. Richard Parker, even at his most dangerous moments, only threatens Pi when he himself feels threatened, and the two learn to coexist, even depending on each other for certain things. Elements of the story like the ocean and the sun can be seen as villains, as they posed a fatal treat to Pi at all times by stranding and dehydrating him. However, these two elements might also be seen as benevolent figures since the ocean supplies Pi with food and the sun keeps him warm and dry. The crew, who are described as drunks by Pi later in the novel, could be seen as villains since Pi points out that their drunken habits might be the cause of the boat's sinking or the animals' escape.)*

6. Do you think Pi's first tale, the one we have come to know throughout the novel, is true? Why or why not? What do Pi's stories suggest about the power and value of storytelling? *(This is the crux of the novel, in a sense. While the major themes are survival and dependence on faith, the question facing the reader at the novel's end is: Which story is true? While the novel forces the reader to make certain leaps of faith, Pi tells the story so fluidly and in such detail that it is easy to believe that the first story is true. However, once Pi tells the second story, the author introduces doubt. As horrific as the second story is, the tale is quite believable as well. It should be noted that when the second tale is finished, Pi asks the men if there is anything about the tale that they would like him to change, hinting that the second story is an invention. Pi never offers to alter the events of the first story. Even so, Pi states that all stories told are stories of invention, so both could be true for a variety of reasons. The author makes it possible to believe that either tale could be true. The fact that Mr. Okamoto and Mr. Chiba choose to believe the first story attests to the value of storytelling. Though not all stories may be true, the details are irrelevant so long as the story is good and reveals something valuable about life. Just as different religions are different lenses through which to see the truth, Pi's stories reveal the truth in different ways.)*

7. In regard to Pi's second story, how does each animal represent its human counterpart (e.g., the French cook and the hyena)? *(Answers will vary. The French cook and the hyena are representative of one another in a few ways. Pi says each has disgusting eating habits and will consume nearly anything, both have foul attitudes, both are dirty and crude, and both are crafty and dangerous butchers. The Chinese sailor and the zebra are alike in that they are both majestic beings writhing in pain, helpless against stronger predators, and unable to communicate their pain to anyone nearby. Pi's mother and Orange Juice are very similar in that both have a motherly aura about them, both are peaceful beings who are vegetarians, and both show great courage in facing their predators but are outmatched and eventually killed. Pi and Richard Parker are alike in that they each lay low at first, letting events happen as they may, but when the cook [or hyena] goes too far, they spring into action and let their ferocious instincts take over.)*

8. Pi knows that each animal has particular habitat needs that must be met while living in a zoo. How does Pi meet (or try to meet) all of Richard Parker's needs while aboard the lifeboat? *(Answers will vary. By using the tarpaulin and the bench as territory borders, Pi splits the available space with Richard Parker. The tarp offers shelter from the sun as well. They each have something akin to privacy, a key need for any animal to feel comfortable. Pi uses the solar stills and the rain catcher, as well as some of the canned water, to fill a bucket [or "watering hole"] for the tiger. Pi also mixes some of the fresh water with seawater because it will make the water last longer and the tiger can handle a little seawater in its diet much better than a human can. Pi feeds Richard Parker as often as he can, sometimes going without food himself in order to do so. He catches fish and turtles, giving the biggest portions to Richard Parker. By sacrificing, working hard each day, and using his extensive knowledge of animals, Pi is able to care for most of Richard Parker's needs.)*

9. Examine the role of love in *Life of Pi*. *(Answers will vary. Love appears in the novel in a variety of ways. Pi obviously loves his family and mourns their loss deeply throughout his journey. Pi also feels great love for Orange Juice when she stands up to the hyena and thumps him on the head. Pi also loves Richard Parker, though he fears him greatly. Pi shouts out loud to Richard Parker that he loves him and will never give up on him. He needs the tiger more and more with each passing day. The tiger gives him a reason to live and becomes something akin to a brother. When Richard Parker lopes into the jungle without saying goodbye, Pi despairs because he truly loves Richard Parker. Pi loves God as well, in any way, shape, form, or practice. He suffers through hardship and scolding in order to love his God. Pi loves villains as well, simply because they are human. When the blind French cook nears Pi's boat, Pi calls the man "brother" and expresses great joy and love for the man. Even when the man tries to kill him, Pi tries to warn him that Richard Parker is nearby. When the man is dead, Pi mourns the loss, proving that Pi is a devout pacifist who loves and values life.)*

10. What do you think is the key element that helped Pi stay alive during his journey? Why do you think this? *(Answers will vary, but students should be able to point to a variety of reasons. Richard Parker is one of them. Pi says that he owes Richard Parker "more gratitude than [he] can express" [p. 361] and that he wouldn't have survived without him. The tiger is his constant companion who gives him a reason to live. He spends his days caring for the tiger's needs, training the tiger, even talking to the tiger. Richard Parker becomes Pi's whole world, and having a purpose is what helped Pi stay focused on survival. Others may say Pi's faith in God is the key factor. Pi often says he turns to God and puts himself in God's hands. He prays every day and thinks of God whenever he is afraid or grateful. His strong faith gives him the fortitude and courage to survive. Thoughts of his family also help him stay hopeful, especially in the days just after the ship sinks. Even long after, when the huge cargo ship nearly plows into them, Pi thinks the ship will rescue him and bring him to his waiting family. A part of Pi knows this will never happen because they are dead, but he lets himself believe, always hoping for the best. Pi's knowledge of animals is a huge factor in his survival. If he was not able to train Richard Parker and live with him, the tiger may have attacked him within the first few weeks. Pi's adaptability and industriousness also are key factors in his survival. Without adapting to life at sea, eating uncommon [and normally, to Pi, detestable] things, and learning how to survive with his meager tools and the survival guide's techniques, Pi would have died within weeks.)*

11. What is the significance of the 100 chapters the novel contains? *(The structure of the novel speaks to Pi's character. Pi is "a person who believes in form, in the harmony of order" [p. 360]. He even dislikes his nickname since the number represented by the mathematic symbol "π," or pi, goes on forever—no beginning, no end. Pi believes in concluding things properly, whether it is one's life, a conversation, a letter, or a last goodbye with a Bengal tiger. Otherwise you are left with only unsaid words and remorse for never having said them. Pi believes people should give everything in life a "meaningful shape" when they can.)*

Post-reading Extension Activities

Writing

1. Write a poem about one of the characters, omitting the name. Exchange poems with a classmate, and attempt to identify the character in the poem you receive. For examples of poetic styles, ask your librarian or teacher for books of poetry to read and review.

2. Write a two-page journal entry for Pi that shows his thoughts after the two Japanese men leave the hospital.

3. Choose an event from your life that changed you, and explain in a two-page essay how you might build a novel around that event. Where would the event take place, what characters would you use, and what would be your main message?

Reading

4. Read a professional book review of *Life of Pi*, and write a one-page response either agreeing or disagreeing with the critic.

Film/Drama

5. Watch one of the following films, and give a presentation (using a clip from the film) to compare and contrast the themes and events in the film with those in the novel: *Lifeboat* (1944), *Lord of the Flies* (1963 or 1990), *Cast Away* (2000), or another "castaway" film. Which do you think most accurately depicts the life of a castaway, and why?

6. Cast your own actors for a film version of *Life of Pi*. Use the character list in this guide as a basis. Choose an actor for each character, and explain your choices in a paragraph for each. The characters do not necessarily have to be of the same nationality as the characters in the novel, but you must explain how and why they exhibit the same traits and ideals.

7. In groups, choose a scene from *Life of Pi* and perform the scene for the class. Be sure to use appropriate props and costumes. (Note: Teachers should monitor the scenes chosen to ensure they are appropriate to be performed.)

Art

8. Choose a character from the novel, and paint a picture or create a collage with images, symbols, and/or words that represent that character's importance in *Life of Pi*.

9. For each section of the study guide for *Life of Pi*, choose a symbol that represents the major action or tone of that section. Create a poster with your symbols, and present your artwork in class.

10. Create either a triple-box comic strip or a single-box comic with a caption based on a humorous or ironic scene from the book. Try to capture the "feel" of the scene in your comic.

Assessment for *Life of Pi*

Assessment is an ongoing process. The following ten items can be completed during study of the novel. Once finished, the student and teacher will check the work. Points may be added to indicate the level of understanding.

Name _____ Date _____

Student   **Teacher**

_____   _____   1. Write a one-page essay explaining which character you can relate to most in *Life of Pi*.

_____   _____   2. Complete the Story Map on page 35 of this guide.

_____   _____   3. Choose 20 vocabulary words from this guide, and write a two-page synopsis of *Life of Pi*.

_____   _____   4. Write four review questions about the novel, and participate in a class oral review.

_____   _____   5. Write a one-page description of one conflict in the novel including whom it involves, how it develops, and how it is resolved.

_____   _____   6. Look online for interviews with Yann Martel, and write a one-page commentary on the interview.

_____   _____   7. Write an acrostic poem about a character or theme from *Life of Pi* using either the character's name or one of the following words: religion, survival, Pondicherry, or Pacific.

_____   _____   8. Complete the Character Chart on page 36 of this guide.

_____   _____   9. Write a review for *Life of Pi* explaining what you liked and/or disliked about the novel.

_____   _____   10. Correct all quizzes taken over the course of reading *Life of Pi*.

Word Map

Directions: Complete the word map below for six of the following words: anecdotes, exemplary, indolence, yogis, anemic, incessant, raiments, proffered, tremulous, intuitive, disrepute, strenuous.

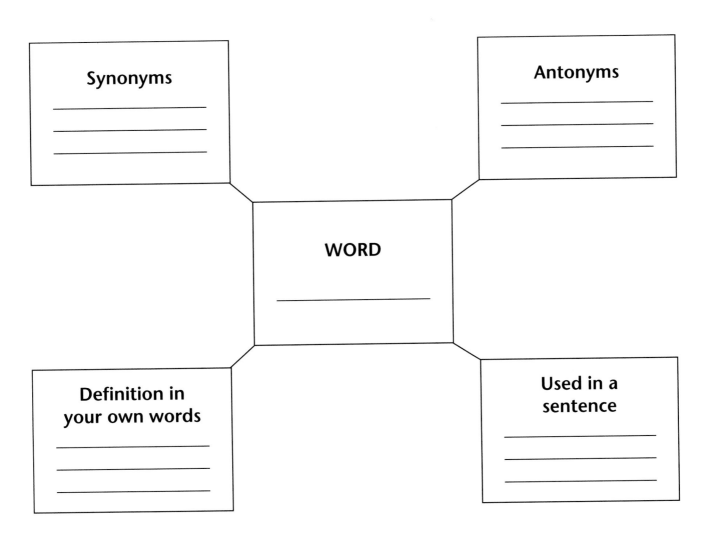

Pros and Cons

Directions: List the positive and negative aspects of having an unusual name.

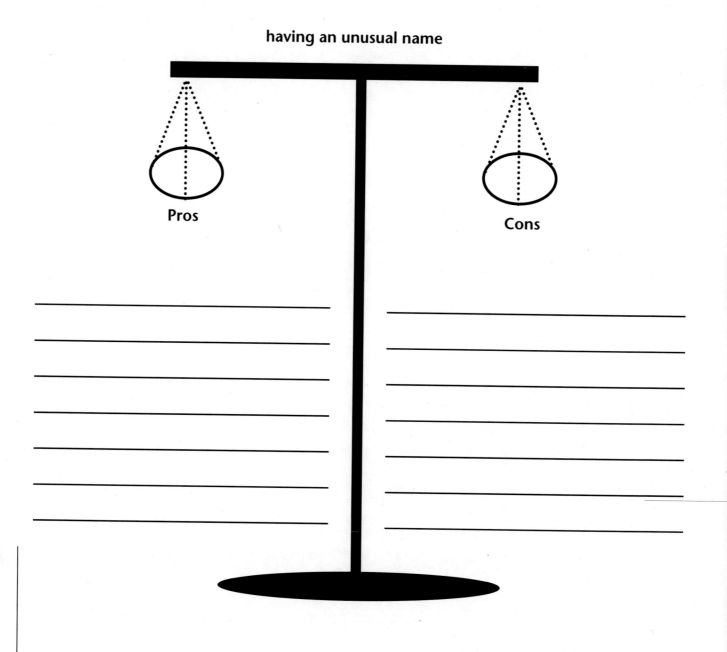

having an unusual name

Pros

Cons

Sociogram

Directions: On the "spokes" surrounding each animal or character's name below, write several adjectives that describe that character. How does one character influence another? On the arrows joining one character to another, write a description of the relationship between the two characters. Remember, relationships go both ways, so each line requires a descriptive word.

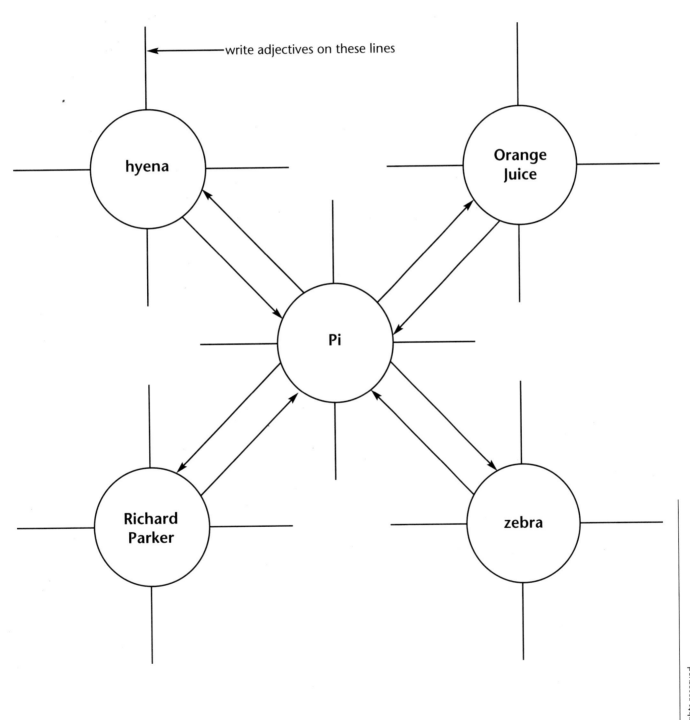

write adjectives on these lines

hyena

Orange Juice

Pi

Richard Parker

zebra

Thought Bubble

Directions: In the bubble below, write what Pi might be thinking when Mr. Okamoto tells him he would like to hear a story without "invention."

Story Map

Directions: Complete the story map below for *Life of Pi*.

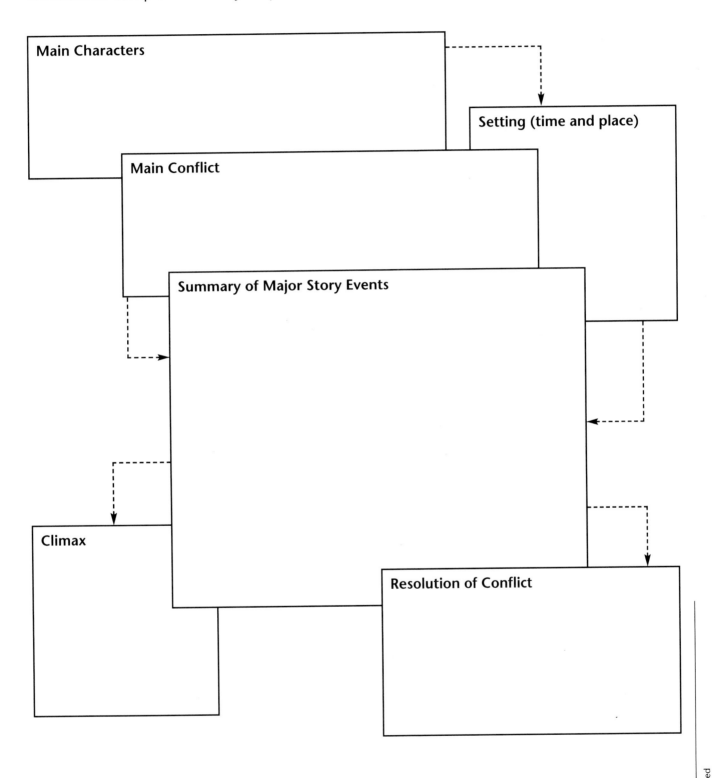

Main Characters

Setting (time and place)

Main Conflict

Summary of Major Story Events

Climax

Resolution of Conflict

Character Chart

Directions: In the boxes across from each of the feelings, describe an incident or time in the novel when each of the listed characters experienced that feeling. You may use "not applicable" if you cannot find an example.

	Pi	Richard Parker	Pi's father	Mr. Okamoto
Frustration				
Anger				
Fear				
Humiliation				
Relief				
Triumph				

Linking Novel Units® Lessons to National and State Reading Assessments

During the past several years, an increasing number of students have faced some form of state-mandated competency testing in reading. Many states now administer state-developed assessments to measure the skills and knowledge emphasized in their particular reading curriculum. The discussion questions and post-reading questions in this Novel Units® Teacher Guide make excellent open-ended comprehension questions and may be used throughout the daily lessons as practice activities. The rubric below provides important information for evaluating responses to open-ended comprehension questions. Teachers may also use scoring rubrics provided for their own state's competency test.

Please note: The Novel Units® Student Packet contains optional open-ended questions in a format similar to many national and state reading assessments.

Scoring Rubric for Open-Ended Items

3-Exemplary	Thorough, complete ideas/information Clear organization throughout Logical reasoning/conclusions Thorough understanding of reading task Accurate, complete response
2-Sufficient	Many relevant ideas/pieces of information Clear organization throughout most of response Minor problems in logical reasoning/conclusions General understanding of reading task Generally accurate and complete response
1-Partially Sufficient	Minimally relevant ideas/information Obvious gaps in organization Obvious problems in logical reasoning/conclusions Minimal understanding of reading task Inaccuracies/incomplete response
0-Insufficient	Irrelevant ideas/information No coherent organization Major problems in logical reasoning/conclusions Little or no understanding of reading task Generally inaccurate/incomplete response

Glossary

Author's Note–Chapter 14

1. anecdotes: stories passed down from one's personal life
2. exemplary: ideal; excellent; of the highest standard
3. indolence: slothfulness; not making any effort
4. yogis: spiritual teachers
5. anemic: weak; lacking energy or vigor
6. incessant: relentless; continuing at the same level
7. raiments: attire; costumes; clothing
8. proffered: given as an offer; extended
9. tremulous: shaking from nervousness
10. intuitive: inherently known; known by instinct
11. disrepute: the loss of a good reputation
12. strenuous: difficult; exhausting

Chapters 15–36

1. sanctified: consecrated; made holy
2. intolerable: unpleasant; so bad it cannot be endured
3. avatar: a representative of one's self/body/ideals
4. petulant: ill-tempered; cranky in a childish manner
5. exaltation: feelings of intense, uplifting joy
6. askance: with doubt or suspicion
7. apoplectic: furious; enraged
8. esplanade: a long, level area, often by the sea
9. depravity: state of moral corruption; wicked act
10. precarious: risky; unsafe
11. memorabilia: objects with personal value or historical importance
12. incredulous: skeptical and unbelieving

Chapters 37–52

1. dyspeptic: acidic; rancid; foul
2. ensconced: made or kept comfortable for a long stay
3. flotsam: floating debris and garbage
4. aversion: avoidance due to great loathing
5. dishevelled: ragged and unkempt
6. remonstrations: strong, forceful arguments
7. empathy: an understanding of the feelings of others
8. abomination: something atrocious, vile, or repulsive
9. empirical: realistic; based on observation or experience
10. supplication: a plea; a passionate request
11. catchment: a reservoir for collecting water

Chapters 53–65

1. lucidity: clarity or understanding
2. lithesome: flexible; able to move gracefully
3. attrition: a wearing down or weakening of resistance
4. mantra: a frequently repeated expression or idea
5. unerring: free of mistakes; sure
6. brackish: somewhat salty

7. galleon: a large, three-masted sailing ship
8. evanescent: fleeting; short-lived
9. sentient: conscious; capable of perception or feeling
10. sanguinary: bloodthirsty; eager to kill
11. mutinous: planning to overthrow someone of authority

Chapters 66–86
1. tilaks: Hindu marks worn on the forehead as symbols of the divine
2. translucent: see-through; transparent
3. forbearance: patience; self-control
4. misconstrue: to get the wrong impression; to misunderstand
5. malaise: listless state; state of depression
6. pendulum: a hanging weight that swings back and forth in a timed pattern
7. gregarious: social and unreserved
8. hillocks: a series of small hills
9. archipelago: a chain of islands
10. heinous: shockingly evil or wicked
11. exalted: lifted up; glorious; most holy

Chapters 87–93
1. emaciated: thin from starvation or illness
2. infernal: unpleasant; annoying; appalling
3. sacrilegious: to treat something holy with deep disrespect
4. amoral: having no morals or ethics
5. famishing: inducing food cravings
6. eviscerated: disemboweled; having the internal parts removed
7. commensal: type of relationship where one party benefits without harm to the other
8. vagaries: fluctuations; variances
9. symbiotic: a mutually beneficial relationship
10. conjecture: to speculate or make a guess
11. deprivation: the state of being without or stripped of all things
12. bereft: filled with a sense of loss

Chapters 94–100
1. surreptitiously: done in a secretive or sneaky manner
2. pliable: easily molded and flexible
3. ruminants: hoofed animals with multiple stomachs (e.g., cows, camels, and giraffes)
4. feral: wild and untamed
5. scimitars: curved blades used by Arabic warriors
6. factuality: a state of truth
7. reprieve: pardon or acquittal; halting of punishment
8. bestial: brutish; lacking human manners
9. impressionistic: giving a general idea rather than details
10. unparalleled: unmatched; beyond comparison

Notes